Bend in the Road

A Collection of Rhymes

I0170629

George Winter

BEND IN THE ROAD

Copyright © 2021 George Robert Winter

All rights reserved.
This book, or parts thereof, may not be reproduced in whole or in part without written permission from the publisher, other than "fair use" as brief quotations embedded in articles and reviews.

ISBN: 978-1-951104-03-0 – Paperback Edition
ISBN: 978-0-9722497-7-5 – Large Print Edition
ISBN: 978-1-951104-11-5 – Hardcover Edition

Cover design and interior layout by Bryce Winter

SP
SAME PAGE

Published by Same Page LLC
www.SamePagePublishing.com

DEDICATION

To my family, and to my mom and dad, (Lena and Robert Winter) and to all our neighbours in Heatherdown, for they were all Alberta pioneers.

George Winter

CONTENTS

PREFACE

POETRY AND TRUTH

According to Shelley, a poem is the image of life expressed in its eternal truth. Eternal truth? Not always!

T.S. Eliot argues that poetry is not the assertion that something is true but the making of that truth more fully real to us. Is that really possible? Take the pain and the description of it—which is more real? Even great description falls short of reality.

Ezra Pound gets closer: poetry is the synthesis of hyacinths and biscuits. No comment. Pound thus uses a poem to define poetry.

In fact, it is much more realistic to contend that poetry owes no allegiance to truth whatsoever. Most poems are not literally true, do not expound a true principle, and make no claim to be absolute reality. Poems do not refer to data, do not claim scientific integrity, and are not peer reviewed.

Poems are about horse feathers, Ladies of Shallott, and lies while lying in someone else's bed. Poems derive from the narrative tradition in which exaggeration is requisite of the audience.

Robert Frost is onto an essence of poetry when he says, '[You] never get over it. Once heard, a good poem achieves permanence. If I may translate into vernacular, poems are earworms. Once they get you, they gotcha.

Katherine Mansfield seems to be on cloud nine when she calls [great] poets the ones with whom she wants to live. But if this means poets enlarge and intensify life, she is onto it.

Samuel Johnson finds the essence of poetry to be invention to produce surprise and delight. But this misses the mark, since a poem cannot surprise on endless repetition—yet repetition is one of the essences of enjoyment.

NOTE ON LANGUAGE: The language of the King James Bible is the most powerful language I know.

This quotation is from Ruth's speech to her mother-in-law, Naomi.

> Whither thou goest I will go
> Thy people shall be my people
> And thy God my God
> And whither thou diest I will die.

COUNTRY LIFE

SHOULD I HAVE BEEN A COWBOY?

Halfway through life a scholar wondered
Should he have chosen a life less grand?
Perhaps it would have been less blundered
If he'd been: just a cowboy on the land.

What if he could start all over?
A haunting thought: a debating stand.
A mix of dream with discontent flow-over.
Just a cowboy on the land.

He sought a place to think things over,
A place alone by waterside.
Where he'd been: the Cliffs of Dover?
No! A place of thought, not suicide.

With this bent he went fly-fishing,
Alone in darkness, in the fall.
Before the sun had waters dancing,
Before the ice formed over all.

His route lay across a pasture
Through a wire fence and wood
To a trout stream that came after
He had fished there since childhood.

As he bent through a fence of wire
In darkness the fauna changed.
Grass became shrubs, there'd been no fire
The cows had modified and so arranged.

A thought touched his conviction:
The fence for cows fenced cowboys equally.
It was, he thought, a cowboy connection
I'd have been good; a cowboy of quality.

At the stream, a breath of magic mist
In night-light still the water did enshroud.
The eerie place in darkest gothic list:
Called to look behind and talk out very loud.

He blessed his lure with wonderment
With a form of magic it was thus endowed.
He hooked something big or sediment
It went deep—fish or spirit, he was cowed.

Clinging thus he felt the line throbbing.
Hand on his rod, feeling for a magic code.
A message for him or for Alan Turing?
He stepped forward, to find a translation mode.

He slipped and fell to a cowboy fate.
 Into freezing water, still grasping for the line.
The message he could now translate:
"Nothing's perfect, nothing divine".

Start life again, could it be better?
The answer to the scholar supine:
His freezing clothes implied the answer,
"Nothing's perfect, nothing divine".

The sun now up a huge red bird
With waters sparkling to bemuse.
The messages in daylight seemed absurd,
even when they came in twos.

He had no fish; he'd had a fright.
He yet clung to one thing that was sure.
Though truth changed from day to night
A cowboy's life was not the cure.

EARED GREBES

Eared grebes had settled in to stay
With tufted head and floating nest
Some had eggs guarded in a bay
The herring gulls came without request.

My canoe without sound I scull
Among the grebes and nest
Swooping low the wheeling gull
Seemed nothing but intrusive pest.

Drifting close, silent my canoe
Scared a grebe from off her nest
The wheeling gulls changed their venue
Gobbling eggs as if they got 'em by bequest.

The quiet scene exploded fast
The gulls could move so quick
The grebe defenses did not last
My guilt, as party to a dirty trick.

The grebes gave up a year of gain
The gulls in breakfast confessed no shame.
In later years I looked in vain
The grebes did not come back again.

ROOSTER

Cock thought himself big boss of the barnyard.
With bright red comb and giant wattles too.
He would chase small creatures very hard
Then brag about it with his crowing crew.

The boy was young and small and timid.
The cock pecked him when he found his back.
It was wrong that fowl could win, and he was livid.
Was there a way that he could build up what he lacked?

Boy hid a stick inside his shirt and postured
Soon cock behind him planned a peck
He pulled the stick and struck, and cock was tutored
Cock ran and boy chased ready to attack.

We know there are many laws of nature
Bigger wins, older wins, stronger wins,
And every law exemplified by some creature
Boy champions that best law of them all: smarter wins.

MAMMALIAN NATION

The sound so loud that one must heed,
for crying out like this reflects a need.
Twenty heifers calling loudly, facing in
An explosive sound from the herd within

I ran to see what had gone wrong.
Was this some kind of warning song?
Danger; perhaps a neighbour's hound.
How account for this loudest sound?

As I got close, I knew the sound,
a bovine cry to gather round.
I'd heard this bellow and seen big cows fly
in united response to a tiny calf's cry.

Finally, pushing and shoving and breathing thin,
I reached the core where they all faced in.
They were licking a fawn and bawling.
It's for the mother they must be calling
The tiny deer could hardly stand
So many midwives with such big tongues
licking it into life, and bellowing like a band.

I picked it up, its ribs pumping as it filled its lungs.
They let me carry the fawn away.

After posing for pictures, the tiny fawn was gently hidden in the bush near where it had been rescued. By next morning its mom had come and it was gone.

The heifers responded to some sound beyond my ears or some smell I could not receive. Or perhaps my body received the message, but my conscious mind did not.

What motivated this splendid demonstration of caring within the mammalian nation?

Was it just mother's sympathy, pheromones? A similar cry of infant distress? I would like to think there are untapped reservoirs of caring and understanding across species of mammals around us.

ECOLOGY AND MY CAR

Too often have I sped through night
Oblivious to the carnage and the bite
For my car kills with thunderous might
Smearing lives as wax on window
Hammering road animals flat and slight
While I pretend I do not know.

No doubt these beasts were in the way
For driving fast or making hay
Like us, they sought to spend the day
And use what's there to reproduce.
Steer round earth's creatures when you may
Or suddenly you're betrothed to moose.

REQUIEM TO A SPIDER

Spider's slender web on car door built
Sparkles as the sun's rays tilt
While tiny dewdrops wave and lilt.
I break through with little thought
Obeying life's agenda without guilt
Believing this is not my dying spot.

How is it spider you have mastered math?
How build a web beyond my engineers by half?
I've broken it and earned your wrath.
Now you'll have to build again
Before December yields its wrath
And immerses us both in freezing pain.

But Spid' y I intend no harm
I've miles to drive; acres to farm.
Why not build against the barn?
My car door's constantly on the go
Too late to send you an alarm
Too late to protect you from the snow.

Spid' y spare me one last thought
The world is more by others wrought
And still others will have bought
the roads and skies for personal leisure.
And so like you I'm tightly caught
Obedient to another's pleasure.

FAIRIES IN MY GARDEN

There are fairies in my garden
Well, butterflies at least.
From my kitchen curtain
I can't tell bugs from beast.

A tiny stone man in hat and leaves
Peers out from behind the hydrangeas
He has his own set of beliefs
But never talks to strangers.

I discussed fairies with the stone man
His voice is record low
He thinks the ferries need a van
Protecting them from snow.

The fairies need that special place
Where the carrots are in clover
To stretch their wings and powder their face
But the carrots won't move over.

SHIFT CHANGE IN THE BARNYARD

Rollback the morning, rooster still asleep
Calves dose while moms already graze
The rams awake but lambs cannot yet leap
Owl coasts to a sleeping branch so silent to amaze.
Brown moths disappear into a spruce bark haze.
And all around the sound of life so blest
Yawning to awake or settling down to rest.

BEND IN THE ROAD

Lights bend around some object on the road
On their dark route to old Makassar
Motorcycles, and trucks with heavy load
Bicycles, and many the foreign car
Around some object on the road.

A boy unconscious there, in the dark, limbs askew.
"Mati, mati,"—Dead, they said when traffic stopped.
And forced to look anew,
Most drivers silent gawked.
Waiting for their journey to renew.

He was young and handsome
Naked, save for brief red shorts
No pockets and no sign where he came from
Barely breathing yet no bloody parts
"Tidak mati," but no ambulance would come.

"Does anyone know a hospital?"
A woman from a small Toyota:
"I know a place," I heard her call.
His chances small as an iota,
'Mati' surely, soon to fall.

Several motorists helped load him
Into the woman's car. Off she went.
It seemed to us the lesser sin
Crowd dispersed, road no longer bent,
The quest for life replaced by traffic din.

Oh! Somewhere there's a mom.
And somewhere there's a dad.
We don't know where they're from
Nor what happened to their lad.
But somewhere there's a mom.

Note: From an experience in Indonesia in 1978. We were near the old city of Makassar, now renamed Ujung Pandang. "Mati mati" means "Dead dead" in Indonesian, and "Tidak mati" means "Not dead."

GAME TRAILS

The game trail has seen the passing of the buffalo
game trails cut by centuries of hoofs
Since Richard led crusades
though moss may be knee-deep.
Some were replaced by wagon roads
Then built into car-friendly gravel
And finally, autobahn and turnpike without limit

But here and there the knee-deep game trails
Intersect the turnpike, and there
The creatures pay the toll of entitlement.

FAMILY

SHE LOVED HIM SO

She reached out with the back of her hand
And slowly stroked his cheek a single time
As though it were a magic wand
Could force life back into him

I saw then that she loved him so
She'd never let me see before
And now she could not let him go
And stood crying there for evermore.

How many times had I seen him reach out
While she with haughty look demurred
Waiting while fate turned dreams to doubt
Leaving her intentions ever deferred.

MOTHER

I often thought while on the lam
Mother should have been a man
Quick to forgive but slow to tan
Please follow if you can.

She could sing 'high C' in a church levee
That's good, you know, for posterity
But just between you and me
Her voice lacked all authority.

Her jaw was rounded if you care
Not powerful and sure, not square
She never developed an effective glare
Moreover, she was short of facial hair.

If I should ever get out of here
I'll go and see the bad old dear
She'll cry and laugh and yes, she'll cheer
With all her faults I love her.

DAD

There is, in Edmonton, a mighty smokestack
standing elegantly alone, looking down on the Coliseum.
Unused, unowned, swaying slightly when the wind is strong.
Fenced for safety, too dangerous to take down,
it has stood thus defiant for half a century.

Beside it once there stood a huge meatpacking house.
Now bankrupt, it is gone like gladiators of old.
So too is my dad; gone since 1958.

Not a big man, but strong and skilled,
he made rowboats. They are all gone:
stolen, rotted, weathered, drowned.

He and his dad built a farmhouse,
barns and a boathouse.
These too are gone.
Moved, dismantled, settled into the ground.
Gone.

But at the bottom of that towering smokestack,
if you know where to look,
you can see marks of a heavy sledge
on the concrete foundation.

The concrete had been badly poured.
My dad, a labourer, had to chip some of it away.
Those sledge marks
are all I can find of his life's work.   *September 2014*

CALM AS A HEADSTONE

"Go out," mom said, through tears,
"But stand well back, don't get in the way."
Unsure if she cried for the horses, or for my dad
struggling to cultivate his potato field, I ran
to where he shouted and swung at Madge,
with a big and heavy chain.
She was afraid of the stoneboat hitched behind.
Did he not see that?

She'd been a family pet, but now, she danced:
Like a child she must obey my dad—Oh! My baby.
She tried but did not know what to do.
So she surged forward and back,
jumping to avoid the chain, bucking
to avoid the stoneboat.
Half a row, half a row,
half a row, on.

As I approached, unseen, dad threw down
the useless chain, and stopped his angry shouting,
He leaned against the broken cultivator, reins
over his arm, and began calmly to roll a cigarette.

Madge was quieting down. He moved to pull
the clevis pin on the doubletree
The stoneboat, unhitched, stayed behind as
he tightened the reins and clicked his tongue.
The team moved forward so smoothly
I wanted to clap.

He stopped and started several times,
then brought them around, picked up the doubletree,
and backed them into the stoneboat. He hooked up,
went back to lean on the cultivator again, calm as a
headstone.

I saw dad now in an unguarded moment:
Hair streaked with grey—I'd never noticed!
Sagging shoulders, bowed head,
wrinkled skin dyed a nicotine yellow,
discouraged and shrunk. But peaceful.
I'd never seen him thus. A sudden revelation:

My dad, strong man,
Loved if frightening
was going to die: to die, to die.

I found myself listening
to a clock strike in the hallway.

The antique clocks of economy
record your every quest
But they take note for eternity,
when you're scheduled to rest.
He saw me as I ran crying to stand beside him
my arms reaching to help.
He began to straighten up.
His body re-inflated;
he became stern and angry again.

And I had almost touched him.

February 2017

NEWLYWEDS

Newlyweds were mom and dad
In a teacherage by a lake
One might think my technique was bad
Or mom's stories were opaque.

She shot a brace of partridge once
In the willows by the shore
Their breast-meat made a tasty lunch
There was a window in the door.

We know just where the schoolhouse was
Some broken walls remain
Enough for most kids and their pappa's
The teacher's kids don't rest the same
Now a century has passed
We can barely reach that far
To seek the mold in which our lives were cast
Look again. The teacherage can't be far.

September 2014

LILY'S SOUL AT MIDLIFE

Down the outside stairs; a girl in a dream
The Danube is blue: step back, twirl now.
Hopping skipping letting off steam.
She'd found her wedding gown: so bow.
She reached the bottom stairs with a bound
The gown was all that remained of her vow.

The gown brought back the laughing years
She danced now, and laughed on the stairs alone.
Before husband's shouts and baby tears.
What could she do without leaving home?

It was 16 dusty miles to town, and she unable to drive.
Hoping for tea with town ladies using all of her charm.
Her marriage gone aground; alone could she thrive?
Rendezvous with town husbands? Alone on the farm?

Her gown would create the required ambience.
Whatever plan, she must get away to town.
To please an imagined bar-stool audience.
She needed to travel, round before sundown.

Up to the "T" she twirled, humming the sound
As though it were a long-lost friend,
In reality this is beyond husband's stated bound;
With her plan one began to understand.
But, sixteen miles to town is beginning not end.
That brown dust, understand, is our eroded land.

Her plan one began to comprehend.
She swung big bosom as she must;
Pumped pedals pushed throttle to its bend
and inhaled a breath of female power.
The Model T, obedient to her lust,
Started rolling, true as a first-time lover.

She seemed to jump and assume command.
'Whoa', she said firmly, but then uncertain—'whoa'.
In a few feet travel, she tried the throttle band.
Nothing worked. Out of incline, it stopped to stand.
She got out, without music, her jiggle—too slow,
The girl's, joy of power: lost in ignored command.

Wearily she climbed back up the stairs,
With a final throbbing sigh, as to say goodbye.
That throbbing, is middle age coming down.
This being a place where no one cares,
She went back, hid her gown, from the prying eye
Back to her joyless husband's judgemental frown.

The Danube is blue, step forward and back,
Reminds me of you; spin round to the right.
Next time Model "T' will do--for me and for you.
Blue gown I'll hide; twirl round, in a sack.
The blue of the Danube is nowhere in sight,
I'm dancing for you-for you; and for me too.

Lily Winter (Bjerke) 1902-1950

Gordon and I sneaked away, knowing we'd accidentally witnessed a very private happening. The poem is based on my observations that day, combined with knowledge of her circumstances.

Lily did not know that her son Gordon and I were watching through a crack in the boards of a shed below the "T."

The Model T was manufactured from 1908 until 1927, but used and broken-down models were available until the early 1940's at low prices. By the 1950's, the old T was beginning to assume value as an antique.

Lily was born in 1902, twin with my dad (twins were celebrated) Grandma and the twins were known across the region. They were beautiful. Lily died of breast cancer in 1950.

I last saw her as we both waited for the street car on 95th Street. She told me through tears that she was going to die.

JOHN

John and I were lads together
Riding by each other's side
Through fair or stormy weather
For me, his purse was open wide.

Then we went our different way
But often messages I'd receive.
Letters sometimes every day
Thoughts to help my happiness reprieve.

When I needed help with seeding
John would come to run the gear.
He could sense when I was needing.
For a day, a month, or year.
When I was short of help to combine
John was there to fix or haul.
As best helper, he would not decline.
For some years, it happened every fall.

Oh! We were lads to together
Riding by each-other's side
Through fair or stormy weather
Today I heard that John had died.

John Pearce 12-05-1926 to 11-02-2011

EDITH

Old beyond her years
With cancer and blind eyed
She sat and smiled through other's tears
The medicine her hair and skin had dried

Someone kindly asked her——a new reporter
"You married twice, I understand."
Her answer showed a wondrous sense of order:
"So far," she whispered behind her hand.

GRANDPA'S LAKE

Lake Mere, the lake where grandpa rented boats for the pennies that he made. The lake was now a weedy slough, with scum, and no tree shade.

In its prime, Lake Mere was a lovely little lake. There was a little store selling farm products in season.

There was a big boat-house, with a heater. It provided protection in the event of a sudden rain or hail-storm. One family had built a cottage for their summer enjoyment. There was a wharf and a line-up of rowboats—everybody had favourites.

There was a big sign Lake Mere just off the municipal dirt road. Driving from Edmonton meant 15 miles of gravel highway and 15 miles of dirt roads and hills mud or dust or snow.

The lake was shaped like a board for Chinese Checkers, with numerous little bays and secret inlets. The locals called it Winter's lake.

One could go fishing using worms and a simple hook. The water was so clear one could see the fish and watch them make a grab at the bait.

In the winter the lake was used for cutting ice to be used in ice hose storage of perishable foods—this in the days before refrigerators.

Oddly I never saw a sail on the lake—perhaps it was too small.

Grandpa had hedges of hollyhocks and caragana. After Grandma died and Grandpa went to Vancouver to live with Dorothy his oldest daughter, the hollyhocks and caragana went wild and spread over the former garden road and yard sites. I was unable to make out if the buildings were burned skidded away or just rotted and fell down. The latter does not seem likely since we found no site of collapsed buildings. The houses were gone, and the new owner pastured his heifers there. Thus, in our search we often encountered big cattle hiding in the bush or running in noisy surprise on sight of us.

We found what may have been the cellar of the old house but did not explore far enough to find the old barn site. Most of what we found relied on our recollections of distance and slope. We had been children, so the distances were smaller than we recalled and the slopes shallower.

Grandma's curtains (where I used to hide, and the grandparents used to pretend they did not know I was there) were grand and thick cloth almost as thick as carpet or pile rug. They slid across to make a separation of the sleeping area from the living room-kitchen. In fact, the cottage consisted of only one room with a curtained barrier across the middle.

Water was the problem. There was no well and no flowing stream or spring. All the water—drinking, washing, and washday had to be laboriously hauled or carried up from the lake. That was a big job and most of the time, there was a horse to do the heavy pulling of a barrel on a stoneboat. But sometimes with no horse available the water had to be carried. It was a short half mile all uphill. (Uphill in both directions.)

Grandma's pies were famous and they both could tuck it away. Grandma would cook pies and then when still hot ask, "Want a piece of pie?" and when he said, "Yes" she would cut the pie in quarters. She gave him one and took one herself.

When that was gone: "Would you like more pie?" And she would pass out the remainder. Thus, in a single sitting they would eat a whole 10-inch pie. With energy supply like that they could well haul up the water.

The house was painted a cheery white with dark trim—very neat and handsome if tiny.

The outside privy was at the far end of the garden. Not far except when it got cold in winter.

Grandpa had a tiny pension from service in the war. It was not much if you bought beer with it, but it bought lots of flour and yeast.

GRANDMA'S HOUSE

And grandma's tiny house was gone
With barn and garden too.
We wept with memories so forlorn
I found a mouldy shoe.

GRANDPA

Grandpa was a drinking man
He bet on horses too.
He was a scrapping man
whom courtesies eschew,
He'd won a boxing prize in Hull.
He worked the trains in the Great War,
Having joined up when he was 48 or 49,
lying about his age. But was injured in a train accident.
He could do one-handed push-ups.

GRANDPA'S GARDEN

He had hollyhocks and strawberries
And cabbage by the score
Corn and hydrangeas and rhubarb
Turnips, radishes and potatoes on the floor

He'd built a cold room to hold ice
On land sloping to the west
And somewhere he had found
A good supply of peat moss

The garden was well fenced on a hill
But the coup de grace was
The exotic birds: guinea hen from Africa
And peacock showing off to everyone.

Grandpa sometimes smelled of beer
Frequently he lacked courtesy and cheer
Doubtless, something in the garden.

PHILOSOPHY

SPY RIDGE

Up the cliff and over the hill
Where highways never run
In dreams, I ride my pony still
In snow in wind and sun.

Up there I ride along the ridge,
Looking down on all the people.
I spy and laugh from that high ledge,
And learn their secrets without scruple.

Once from on high, I saw my dad,
Toting patties to a bin.
Oh! He was a strapping, handsome lad,
Until the cig's got hold of him.

Another time I saw my mother
Working horses with a boy.
I shed some tears, I so loved her.
I lie to call them tears of joy.

And now I ride to ridge's end,
Alone save for my pony.
And though she was my closest friend,
The ridge is desolate and lonely.

Note: patties are potatoes.

SKIPPING ROPE-A-DOPE

Boy riding a bike in winter icy dark
Tried to wheel between two cars following close
He did not see the heavy rope
By which the one pulled the other
He had barely time to get through
But could not skip the rope.

September 2014

GETTING OUT

I did not ask to come in here,
this place of hunger and of fear.
I did not tell you: "lock the door,
and hold me prisoner evermore."

My mother pushed me down this lane.
Her lovely face was racked with pain.
She stayed a while though we all knew.
Her wondrous strength was weakness too.

But she at least must know the route,
And what life without is all about.
Like her, I'd vanish without a trace:
escape my wrinkles, quit the chase.

If I could find the key, we'd see:
Who can stop me as I flee?
But I would not know the way,
perhaps I'll wait another day.

May 2011

FINDING DARKNESS

"Forget your perfect offering
There is a crack in everything
That's how the light gets in."

Cohen is correct beyond a doubt
Cracks spill the darkness out
Shadows fade all round about.

City borders shown by night
Man's dominion marked by light.
Could Edison's genius turn and bite?

Light is the gas pedal of our fate.
Frenetic lightings titillate
No way to slow or even wait.

Darkness has become a fable
Control our speed? We are not able.
We could dance right off the table.

Perhaps you know a country site
Where stars exist despite man's light
There you will enjoy the night.

Slow down; turn up the dark!

With recognition of Leonard Cohen.
October 09, 2013

APPROACHING MANHOOD

From the awful verge of manhood
Their paths diverge by chance
And some will strive to do good
And some will simply dance.

A few seek riches too soon
by sawing down the wood
or gun a species to its doom.
or fish to extinction, 'cause they could

Then the verge of manhood passes
Replaced by verge of old
They regret the buffalo passage
The loss of whales, and empty mines of gold

But who is seeking balance
Between the verges now
Between those who act too quickly
And those who've learned not how?

HEADLINE: NOT PUBLISHED

A boy. Looking for game with rifle
Started cross the big frozen river
As a shooter, he should have been
out of town. But no one in sight.
Halfway over he crossed
A sewage outfall!
He stopped when to his surprise
he saw big chunks of sediment roiling in the water
through glass-thin ice at his feet.

Not prepared to turn back, he turned downstream.
One step, two, then he went through.
The little rifle hung up front and back on the ice.
The current pulled at his body.
The rifle, in his armpit, held.
Death he knew waited in the strong current
inches away. He trusted the rifle.
With one hand on the rifle and one on the ice
He scrambled out soaked in effluent,
and treading lightly ran back the way he had come
upstream, around the glassy ice, and across.

No one sent the story to the newspaper:
"Two weeks since boy disappears. No trace…"

GROWING UP WITH HORSES

TINY LOST CORNER OF THE WORLD

Lena was a small woman and she laughed when I brought out the three-legged stool from the milking stall. But she stood on it and brought big Madge alongside. Then, quick before I could do anything more, she grabbed the mane and leaped— belly down on Madge's broad back. And brought a leg over till she could sit up—one leg on each side and no saddle. Madge knew her and there was no objection. The small woman was boss; Madge and I both knew that.

I was on Lady, the old gray Percheron, just bare-back and without even a bridle, as we set off. The horses had worked all day but were anxious to get to the creek for water, so they were brisk in a long-striding walk. Madge led, Lady followed. Since horses follow the leader and don't like the ambiguity of side-by-side, so I could not talk to Lena.

Madge had an infected wound on her shoulder. It was exuding a white bloody pus and would not heal—perhaps irritated by the harness. And so Lena had decided we would go to see George Welsh.

Welsh was a rancher now. Once a cowboy, he did "trick roping" putting on a show at every community picnic. He was a magician with a rope. He had once put on a show for visiting royalty, where he met the Queen. I too had seen the King and Queen as they "united the Empire" back in '39 before the war. The King and Queen showed themselves on Edmonton's Portage Avenue now called Kingsway as we sat on makeshift seats along their route.

Welsh was no doubt famous in our small corner of the world. More to the point, he was a knowledgeable and experienced horseman.

It was seven miles to his ranch, so it would take us about four hours round trip.

Lena passed me a thick sandwich as we sat our horses at the creek. And I pointed out to her the place where Lady and I had gone in over our heads when I inadvertently tried to cross at a wash-out. Lady had been reluctant, but I had urged her on and she reached out with both front feet. She could find no solid ground, and could not turn back, so we had both toppled in and under.

It was a time, in our small corner before telephones, so Welsh could not know we were coming. We had no costly radio and television had not yet been invented. We did not subscribe to a newspaper—that cost money.

We crossed the stream and went along the railway spur to the grand old gravel crusher.

The rail and crusher were part of a bankrupt system that supplied crushed gravel for the construction of Edmonton's High Level Bridge and the Parliament Buildings (1913). Now it was a ghost hole in the ground with a locomotive that had gone off the tracks and killed the engineer. There remained a great towering crusher that once sorted and crushed but now stood silent. Not far away were rail-mounted steam loaders, looking just as ready for work as they had the day when the operators had gone off-shift many years ago.

Lena told me again to stay away from the dangerous collapsing cedar wood crusher, as I wondered again about the businessmen who had owned it all, before the grand collapse in the Great Depression.

We passed through the sand dunes where sand had washed out of the mining effluent, and I told her about Ted and Don and how walking through the clumps of willow, I had terrified everyone including myself by threat of "Pollock's bull" —so that we fled at full speed twirling and tumbling around the willows at maximum speed. Charlie and Elsie were wealthy and had a car, and told us about the Ministry of Education where Charlie was an important executive.

Welsh was out of the house before we got far into the yard. Lena did the talking, sliding off Madge and walking to meet him. But Welsh saw immediately what needed doing. He invited us to come in the house as he prepared his medication.

I stayed with the horses and he soon came back. He washed out the wound, cut away some proud flesh with scissors, and sutured the wound so it could continue draining. All the while explaining how horses healed differently and would re-grow the flesh he had cut away. Unlike people, he said. Madge stood still and quiet, as though she knew we were helping her. The nice thing was he told me "man to man" what he was doing.

He handed me the little bottle and said, "Twice a day, soak cloth with antiseptic, bathe wound. Don't spill antiseptic. First wash hands. Keep treating it till the antiseptic is all gone."

Lena came out of the house saying good-bye to someone inside. She thanked Welsh but did not offer to pay. She later explained to me, "Welsh knew we had no money. He had none, no one else had money, even ledger in the grocery store just keeps a notebook of transactions."

We said our thanks, mounted and rode back as we had come; back to our tiny corner.

But as Lena later explained: Churchill has called for men from every corner of the Empire to assist in the war against Hitler. Your father is training among troops in some unknown corner of England. "Every corner will do its part," she said, and I understood the royal visit, the abandoned crusher, the sand dunes, and the excavators, even the creek and even Welsh and Madge, even Lena and I, every-one, every-thing must somehow do their part.

THE BIG MARE WAS IN HEAT

The big mare was in heat
She was not coy and not discreet
Wanting the world to know
About her body glow.
Jets of urine marked the times
Like an actress doing mimes.

Capturing the reins under her tail
She would hold them tight and so prevail
Until the driver creating a fuss
Pulling "Gee" or "Ha" provided a stimulus
Thus, she got a form of relief illicit
And tail over reins made us complicit.

RADIO

As you know (of course)
A radio is not a horse
When there's no hay
A horse does not neigh

WILD HORSES ON THE EASTERN SLOPES

Horses, horses, bay black and white
Pawing snorting wild and free
Far from road and city light
Hiding in the mountain night
Where few men can come and see.

We've ridden slowly dawn to dark,
Searching every hidden glade.
My companion topped a hill of mollusk
There before us: bare and stark
A wild stallion had his harem laid.

The stallion up with a single bound
Urging his mares to run and hide
Demanding obedience without a sound
Circling back and going round.
Envy him, you who are denied.

It's a world unto itself, here along the eastern slopes
With grizzly bear and wolverine
Like a wildlife kaleidoscope
Before man with quads and microscope
Before these men could intervene.

Some mares run while others stay to fight
Some are thin, one is blind, and some are lame
Some foals are robust, and some are slight
Could man be horse and yet delight?
Would the wild eyes stay the same?
After a few seconds of dust and drumming hoof
Their fear of us did not seem right.
As quick as a magician's proof
As though they were from man aloof
They are devoured by the night.

I wanted to call out, 'Wait!'
'We mean no harm.'
The explanation came too late
Man's tyranny had been their constant fate
The smell of man triggered their alarm.

In 1980, a horse-loving faculty member at Olds College and I have a ride into the eastern slopes of the Rockies west of Didsbury, Alberta. Starting with horses loaded on a truck, after two hours driving, we offloaded the horses the road being impassable to wheeled vehicles. We rode on west on horseback. We were looking for feral horses and enjoying the wildness.

HORSES WILD AND TAME

Horses, horses, wild and tame
'Speed' shall be thy second name.
But if perchance 'speed' will not do.
Then brave and strong are also true.

Horses, horses black and white
Colors of the day and night.
In ancient time with man you fought,
Until with man you cast your lot.

Horses, horses deep inside
Heart and smart in you reside.
Was it the she-wolf's hunting cry
Brought you to man with whom to die?

Horses, horses, speed and power
Took you to some couple's bower
In centuries gone, woman could see
"She feeds her babies just like me."
Horses, horses, your powerful grace
Was sculptured by the tiger's chase
And those who knew what you had done
Saw that the tiger could be outrun.

Horses, horses, wild and free
If I could I'd be like thee

GONE FROM THE CITY

The small boy sawed the outline of a horse's head
To make a wall decoration for his mom
At Sunday school in the white church
before the country graveyard.

The farm team: Madge and Lady pulled the wagon
Taking the family to the railway station
The boy looked back as they went down the hill
Thinking he would never see their home again.

His mother had written the lonely boy
giving him the young mare: named May,
who he now rode to the country school
Living with Mildred in the war doing the chores.

It was a summer job for a university student,
Driving horse to deliver milk, across the high bridge.
The big gelding 'Jim': so smart—he knew every stop,
He'd skid wheels on curb to brake going downhill.

His daughter's pony: Eclipse: half Welsh, half Arab
Tough, yet gentle, collided with a car one night
The daughter was unhurt, the pony deeply wounded.
She stood quiet while, sans anesthetic, the vet cut and
stitched.

They were his friends, his workmates,
He felt their pain, and they knew his moods
They are gone now from a city, where children
once brought a handful of grass to big smart Jim.

April 16, 2016

TRAVELLING STALLION

Into the farmyard came the great stallion.
The yard buzz fell silent with sucking of the air
Even the worms reared up to stare.
Farm animals touched each other for reassurance
Rooster touched and quieted his exuberance
Children slid under the bed to hide.
The man who 'led' him walked beside.
The coming of the stallion.

Proof of stallion excellence was there for all to see
Address him as "Your Majesty"
Blackening the sky, with unimagined lust,
Like a summer storm contradicting rain with dust.

This storm was a stallion, his power for all to see:
muscles swelling and rolling, eyes flashing
hooves crashing, mouth open and reaching, mane blowing.
His call was yearning but his intentions were clear.
Everything and everyone got out of his way.
Then we turned to see what the King would do.

Dancing, prancing, enhancing, advancing,
calling and erecting his giant penis.
It advertised lust and power promising continuity of his
genus,
but threatening too, threatening all with a torrent of
darkness.

Mrs. N., who had come on business to inspect the poultry,
watched, and unconsciously wrapped her scarf protectively
over her breast and tugged up her skirt. "My God," she
breathed, "Look at that."

The 'stud man', not entirely in control, called out a belated
warning: "No women or children allowed," he said into the
wind.

"Fine," said Mrs. N to her host. "So, I must go.
For poultry inspection there is no fee.
Women not allowed?
I will go before he shoves it into me."

WOMEN

WOMEN IN THE WINDOW

She took you by the hand
to her boat on the water.
And asked you to row across
To the blackbirds on the shore.
The noisy nesting blackbirds on the shore.

You could not see her clearly, but
From her hand you knew.
She was much too young for you
Yet this child had the poise of a woman
A chrysalis ready to emerge as woman.
As you rowed toward the sound
She said, "Y' know my dad is dead."
Then she chatted about the birds
Next moment, her purpose became clear.
"D' you think there is a heaven;
A place for the good people: a heaven?"

You were quiet and the boat glided
into the reeds along the shore
She stepped into the muddy shallow water and ran,
a child looking for answers
On the shore, for blackbirds and her father.

Finally she returned, downcast. She sat
Silent. You began to row. Finally, it was
You who said: "There are things
We cannot know"—you sensed she was studying your
face—"will never know."
"Some things, tis good to never know" she sobbed.
You saw that:
You'd opened a window
A window though you're blind
A window in her mind.
On return, she took your hand again.
"I'll introduce you to my mom."
She led you to a stately woman,
"Mom this is my new boyfriend."
Adult words: but from a child.
Then she ran to play, as would any child.

Mom offered a tea." Wow," you said,
"What energy." "She tires me out," said mom.
"She is only eleven, and too young for a boyfriend."
She laughed.
"Oh my," you laughed with her,
"She is super intelligent—and creates a powerful first
 impression."

Mom said: "She is her father's daughter."
So you knew
You'd opened a window
A window though you're blind
A window in her mind.

Then you spilled your tea.
You blurted, "Oh I'm sorry. I'm quite blind. I'd better go."
Wiping the table, she said, "Please—I guessed the
blindness—don't go. I hardly know you. It's lonely now,
without… Have another cup of tea".
You sat down, "Thanks, I'd like another tea."
And you knew:
She'd opened a window
A window though you're blind
A window in your mind.

WOMAN

Woman, woman breathing fast.
I read your thoughts from glances cast
What goals or dreams long past
Could cause this surging in thy breast?

In what cradle did you rock
Dreaming of some tender look?
On what swing did you once soar
Seeking love for evermore?

With body that's a work of art
Do I dare to seek your heart?
Your mouth your lips your eyes,
Conceal no secrets, tell no lies.

What is driving you so fast?
Did your father set the last?
Does my life fulfill your dream?
Trickles join to form a stream.

When these passions play their course
what will keep us one—what force?
Will you go quietly on your way
Leaving me alone at end of day?

Woman, woman breathing fast,
Find me where your glances cast.
From those goals and dreams long past
Will thy surging bosom last?

June 2014

THE GIFT

A boy and his dad were shopping for a present: a Christmas gift for the boy to give to his mother.

They had moved to Montreal in the fall, and wanting the boy to learn French, his parents had enrolled him at age six in grade two of a French school. But all the French schools were Catholic. The boy had sat in class every day, understanding little of the lesson or ritual of the Catholic nuns who were his teachers. The situation was unusual, English speaking parents without religious affiliation, did not ordinarily put their children in French Catholic schools—particularly not in grade two— where religion is a large component of the curriculum. It was unusual too, that the boy knew exactly what he going to buy for his mother.

They soon found the jewelry section, and the boy identified a long necklace with shiny red glass beads. "This," he said and took a firm hold of it. A nervous clerk began moving toward them. The dad, trying to dissuade the enthusiasm of his son said, "Something like that?" He could see that the bejeweled necklace was in fact a rosary.

The son said, "Yes, the nuns at my school all have one and play with it all the time." Afterward, in mentally running through the events, that led to the big mistake, the dad realized that this was the moment to have spoken up forcefully, 'These are catholic rosaries, mom would not want one.' Or 'No this is not suitable, this has religious meaning and we are not Catholics.' Or simply, 'No this will not do'.

Instead, he pointed to a pearl necklace, which while imitation was far beyond his son's budget. "How about something like this?"

It did not work. The boy had seized onto this particular necklace. It will be beyond his budget too thought the dad. But it was cheap, at only $1.29. 'Probably subsidized by the church,' the dad thought.

They bought it and returned home.

On Christmas day, the mom, duly forewarned, feigned delight, gushed a thanks, and wore the rosary all the rest of the day. After that, it disappeared.

The dad did not see it again until after many years after the messy divorce, after the cancer, which struck down his former wife, and after the final stroke that eventually proved terminal.

He and his son went, one final time to see her. She was comatose, barely breathing, drawing nourishment from feeding tubes. The nurse said: "When the tubes are removed, she will slip peacefully away."

There was nothing they could do. It was too late to even say good-bye. In time they turned to leave.

But something caught his eye, hanging from the bedstead. Red glass beads catching the sun's rays: it was the ancient rosary. She had taken it to bed with her one last time.

The old man reached over and held it for his son to see: "Look," he said.

His son looked for a moment, but without recognition.

"Sorry dad, those gems are just glass."

February 2017

SLIPPING AWAY

Slip away.
She will slip peacefully away.
The nurse had said it: "When
the feeding tubes are removed,
she will slip peacefully away."

But wait: this woman is the mother
of my children and grandchildren.
She can't 'slip peacefully away.'
There is no peace in my heart.

Did you say: 'my heart will have
to find its own peace?' I suppose so.
Yes, I know: there is no going back.
But don't you see, I go back every night;
every dream reviews our past.

"Who decides when to remove the feeding tubes?"
"The doctor consults with members of the family," you say.
"Which members?"
Not me, the divorced husband.
Is thirty-five years married not enough?
I suppose not.

Is it conceivable she hears us now? That she understands?
You think not—but are you certain?
I might say, 'good-bye,' and yes, 'I'm sorry.
Sorry it turned out this way.
Sorry for all the mistakes, the selfish things. Sorry.'

Who is to decide? ...The tubes.
The doctor consult family members.
No, I suppose it does not include me—
the former husband.
Thirty-five years together is not enough.

Good-bye, my love. Good-bye.

ODE TO DOROTHY

The tides of life pass o'er
Leaving sculptured sand along the shore
Sometimes strong and ever clear
At others weak and full of fear.

The sand itself so formed
Redirects the waters flumed
At times it curses at the power
Then uses it to form its bower

Tho' ocean and the shore are one
Don't forget the wind and sun.
For verity it's that sunny face
That locks us all in tight embrace.

ALONE

Wild hopes and youthful dreams
Which I thought had eroded all away
Came back to infect my very seams
And threaten I will break apart someday.

When you were here my love
Rejection always framed my thought.
It pained you as if He from above
Imprisoned us in mystic doubt.

We went our separate ways
Magnets with our fields reversed.
Till years made up of finite days,
And all attempts at friendship cursed.
Until near end, it fell to me
To harvest all the pain and dirt
To see it was not meant to be.
What started joy, had turned to hurt.

And now you've gone, I'm left behind.
To wonder at a world so empty now
It seems the shackles meant to bind
Swung open more with every vow.

January 27, 2016

FOR FUN AND PAIN

NOTHING MORE

A time when innocence we could adore
When mother played the piano softly,
We with happy laughter wasteful pour
Songs down the hall and out the door.

This was how I courted gently,
Singing soft and yet intently,
Laughter filling, joy enough for spilling on the floor.
In this way I wooed a maiden,
You were that maiden.
No one more!

A moment passed. What was in store?
The piano notes delighted evermore.
But we singers were reluctant on the floor.
It seemed we wanted something more
It was then I tasted music's freedom.
While exploring every music kingdom.

This was how mother, you, and me: we three,
Knew joy and laughter as if free.
Notes fulfilling, pure enough to reach the core.
In this way we meld together.
Meld together.
Nothing more.

It seems so long ago, I've nearly forgotten how
Another came between us.
Squandering all our musical genius
He found a way for rain on me to pour
To close me out and lock the door.
He beat you, called you whore.
Then blamed his wicked temper on my family lore.
I've more rage than I have floor,
Anger enough to foment war.
You must have known 'twas you I sang for.
I sang for you.
For nothing more.

TUT WAS HAPPY

King Tut was happy with his thousand sacred cats
And 1,000 dogs named "Spot"
A dozen Egyptian lions not yet shot.
With ox and fox, chickens and eggs,
Birds and squirrels and many slaves
But his golden mask is holed since
He had no camels, no elephants, worse no horses.
Hannibal went one better with 36 fighting elephants
And he had cavalry too, but he had no camels.

MEMORY

Some old folks have memories vast
For times that they enjoyed
With details of a laughing past
Before they were employed

Their siblings who were sometimes there
Recall events quite different
They have to question when and where
Arose a memory so magnificent.

FOLLOW THE BOTTLE

The bottle he'd been hiding was Irish Cream.
He grabbed it now and with his hunting rifle
Rode his quad past dreams that he must stifle
To the little grove of birches by the stream.

Here he searched the quad and found pencil stub.
His pockets yielded tissue paper not too small

He gulped a heavy drink from the Irish pub,
The leaves were cast, the sky was grey; it was fall.

Another gulp
And carefully replaced the cap as though it mattered.

Then scrawling wrote: this note shows I ain't in some pickle.
I'm taking my own life.
Goodbye to my little lass.
My life ain't worth a wooden nickel
Now, the whiskey taking hold, he finished with,
"I'm sorry, for all the failures.
Tell that university asshole, that wasps do control mozzies."

He pumped a cartridge into the rifle chamber,
And wrote a bullet through his head.
The sound so loud was muffled by the trees
Within two seconds he was dead.
His son who found the body, said, "Whiskey it would seem."
His father said, "I'd hoped he'd be a professional man."
His mother recalled that when he was two,
he always banged his head.

His wife went back to work packing groceries.
His daughter screamed; but rescued the Irish Cream.

LURE OF THE SOUTH POLE

You are old Robert Scott, he said with a drawl.
And your hair has become very white,
Yet you incessantly talk of a trip to the pole.
Do you think at your age it is right?

In my youth, Peter, father replied to his son,
I spared not a dime for the ponies.
I believed if I thought it the matter was done.
Real travel was only for phonies.

You are old, father, but surely you know,
That ponies have hoofs and extremely short hair.
Their feet will do nothing but slide in the snow.
Their thin coats will freeze when they're bare.

In my youth, said the sage, I believed what was said.
Now I know something of public relations,
As sleeping buddies, ponies keep a cozy warm bed.
They'll be feted by all delegations.

You are old, said the boy, but surely you see
Animals designed (as it were) for the ice.
While some animals live all their lives in a tree,
A horse's design is not nice.

Was a time, said the wise one, I'd listen and hear
How some things are morally right.
Things that were wrong would ring in my ear.
I could argue this all through the night.

You are old, said son Peter, but think ever deeper,
Of creatures most suited to run.
Tigers run faster but dogs run much cheaper.
But the white bear is enormously fun.

I can see, said the father, your plan has a flaw
It cannot go possibly right.
The bear on my men will sequentially gnaw,
They cannot last through the very first night.

You are old, said bold Peter, your point is so droll.
So long as you travel real quick,
You'll be back from the pole with the bear in a stroll.
The delegates will find it quite slick.

But said his father, you did not explain.
How to avoid the bear's hunger from winning,
If he ate of my men, I'd get all the blame
And delegates praise would be dimming.

It's true said his son. What causes it all,
is that you insist on bad planning.
If you keep on like this from now to the fall,
Not a pony will be right or left standing.

2010

FAILED PATHS

I close my eyes and in dreams recall
Paths others would take where I'd trip and fall.
Seeking to win working hard and steady,
Led me to dangers others knew already.
And looking back I cannot say
I have found good or a better way.
Now I'm old and on paths too late,
So back I go to the dreams I hate.

2010

YOUR DOG RAY

Your dog Ray, the one with the knitted vest
Won't eat till I come home
What strategy do you suggest?

Try to come home sooner
The dog always needs a rest
Perhaps bring him a bone
That would really be best

Your dog Ray
The one with the knitted vest
Barks at me all night long
Have you anything to suggest?

Quit your job at the bank
Sell out and move away
It's not my problem don't you see
And I'm not going to pay.

After Allan Ahberg's "Please Mrs. Butler."

FARMING

JUSTIFYING

We till the soil and plant our seeds,
And dream of harvest without weeds
Add weather pests and goals organic,
It tends to drive us nearly frantic.

Insects galore on crops will dine,
If we're not as smart as old Einstein.
Since pests are not amenable to bribes,
We tend to reach for pesticides.

With pesticides moms cannot 'bide,
So on GMO our hopes reside.

2010

INDUSTRIAL FARM

"No Trespassing" the sign made clear,
But it was Sunday with no guards near.
The boy slipped through the wires quick and light
The smallest sound would cause his flight.
The object of his study was a farm not right.

Trucks were lined up in the potato field,
And gone the lane where the posts were peeled,
There children had run each evening race,
 gone were the stakes marking each child's place.
Where they'd played ball, he found no trace.

He saw a great hole where the house once stood,
It had been a warm home and built all of wood.
The garden and barn site were piles of crushed rock.
A farm family's needs the gravel would block.
An industrialized farm; it came as a shock.

THE OLD WELL

The boy walked down where the road used to be.
And there sheltered behind an ancient spruce tree,
Which measured its age—old enough to sell,
And under the tree in a cozy small dell.
A dimple in the earth had once been a well.

They had kneeled there together, he and his dad,
Looking down to the water and feeling quite bad.
The ladder once nailed there was breaking away,
The casing was spilling big chunks of clay.
The old well would barely last through the day.

Floating boards kept the pail from the water,
They tried rocks in the pail but just crushed it flatter.
Urging the pail past the boards with the rope,
When every piece was as slippery as soap,
Led them to decide the method was broke.

His dad had said: "If I go down and the ladder fails,
I'd never be able to climb up these slippery old rails.
But I could lower you on the rope, you're still small,
Then pull you out against the slippery old wall.
With the rope holding tight, you surely can't fall."

The boy remembered thinking: 'I might die'
And screwed up his face trying not to cry.
He thought: 'this man is full of weakness and fear.'
This big man who was as strong as a steer.
He'd needed to father his dad, which was queer.

But now in earth's dimple, he saw a wider scope.
A father using all his resources, still unable to cope,
His sick wife had brought out all of his fears.
The boy retraced his steps, flooded with tears.
His maligned dad had been dead for over 50 years.

AFTER THE WARMING

WARMING CHANGES EVERYTHING. *Samuel Taylor Coleridge wrote in Kubla Khan: "Where Alph, the sacred river ran, down to the sacred sea." He depicted a different world. Here, I try to write in a corresponding style, stretching to find a different world—one after global warming. The laws of physics may apply, but circumstances change in surprising ways.*

During warming, with melting and swelling the seas grew bigger. Expanding day by day, spilling warm water over the shores and banks of well washed sand; incurring the wrath of the gods of land. Foolish men expected to continue just as before. But warming changed everything.

The seas and oceans overflowed and raging storms immersed low cities. Water drowned ancient monuments, swamping roads, choking airports, immersing docks so ships could neither load nor land.

AFTER THE WARMING

The wind with a resentful stealth
piled up the waves so high
They would have blocked it
had there been a sunny cloudless sky.

The sacred water straight and high,
left nothing for the shore.
And fishing boats for fishermen,
were beached for evermore.

Along the shoreline now exposed,
were walls of squared-off stone.
Some ancient civilization had tarried there,
perhaps it our own.

Many the fish outgrew its scales,
swelling too big to be fried.
Some became as huge as fairy-whales.
too large to sit bestride.

North Wind hated waves for their slope and bevel.
But gargantuan waves she found boring and dry.
She settled instead for a sea smooth and level,
and hence blew all the waves into the sky.

Up there the waves, were dark as a boss's frown.
Giant moving wrinkles across a fat sky's belly,
falling up, and around but never down,
leaving the sea top as smooth as a bowl of jelly.

The sea was sacred, the wind the same,
And now the rivers never ended,
The younger fish could play a different game,
because the water was upended.

The boldest fish played a nipping game,
with everyone—another.
But it was dark, and some were lame,
and (Oh baby brother)!

A small piece was snipped, if with distain.
from Bertha, a large whale's mother.
"Ouch! I'm snipped," she cried in pain.
"You were too cowardly to snip my big brother."

The snip of course was quite unwise.
For, Bertha was divine,
and those who saw her anger rise.
knew it would explode like boiling turpentine.

She could not catch the tiny fish,
For they were quick and ken;
So she began to swallow,
the slow old fishermen.

While no one ever counted,
yet produced in this way
there were 5 or 10 new Jonahs,
5 or 10 raw Jonahs swallowed in a day.

They were not chewed and swallowed,
For Bertha had no teeth.
So she held them in her roof of mouth,
rather just beneath.

The sea had seemed the enemy,
with the flooding of the docks.
But winds had changed the economy,
and shaped the water like a box.

And all the creatures residing there,
had changes their tastes and style.
They'd learned to sleep most anywhere,
and practiced habits to beguile.

The wind with a resentful stealth,
piled up the waves so high,
They would have blocked, it
 had there been a sunny cloudless sky.

The sacred water straight and high
left nothing for the shore.
And fishing boats for fishermen
were beached for evermore.

Along the shoreline now exposed
were walls of squared off stone
Some ancient civilization had tarried there,
perhaps it our own.

A CHILD'S PERSPECTIVE

MUSE OF YOUTH

The Greeks called it the 'muse of youth'
A guiding god whose genius does not fall.
But we and they overlooked a truth,
Innocence, the price of muse, is heinous after all.

A CHILD'S PERSPECTIVE

On shore, the sacred children asked if when
Their sacred fisher dads would be home gain,
And as they constantly grew thinner
would their dads, bring sacred fishy dinner?

A small boy, whose name was Glen,
had a nickname: 'Mighty Mite' or 'Might,'
named for things he might do if he were ten.
He teased his sister, she pretended a fright

Once he said, showing his claws.
He "might spit on his sister's toast."
She believed in Santa Claus.
And left Santa pickles due to that boast.
Dressed in his father's raincoat,
Might went looking for his dad,
Mother tied him to a fish line from their boat.
The line was long, the strongest that they had.
The wind howled, because Might was small.
Mom was afraid he would blow way.
Arms catching the wind as parasol,
Might lifting like a kite twenty times a day.

In fact, Mighty Might was quite scared.
What if he fell? What if Mom blew away too?
The sacred sea was there if he dared.
And some kids were watching—at least a few.

Might was more than a little worried.
Kites could anger Poseidon, god of the sea.
But he was too proud to turn back scared.
He must look for dad wherever he might be.

His mom shouted, "Can you see your dad?"
"Give me more line—more line."
Soon he was far out over the sea so bad.
He was certain he'd find his dad this time.

Below through the wind and rain
His dad was rowing and trying to sail.
Away from, an island? He looked again.
The island resolved—into Bertha the whale.
He landed by a giant whale eye. "Please Mr. "

"Madame" said the whale with a sigh.
"She's not a 'Mr.' She is a lady. She is like
Eve and not like Adam—She is a 'Madame'"
said a dolphin, which was swimming
alongside the island in water of many fathom.

"Oh! I am sorry," Might carefully pronounced.
"Please let my dad go, Madame whale."
"I want a 'No Smoking' sign." Bertha announced.
as though from sadness her logic could fail.

"She hates cigarette smoke," said a dolphin.
Some fishermen she swallowed are smokers,
Another said: "Most smoke, in my opinion."
A third, "It is a big mistake, if anyone cares."

"Who are you? and you? and you?" he asked.
"I'm Bertha's manager," said first with distain,
"I'm chief planner," second stated her task.
"I'm scapegoat," said the third. "I take blame."

"Wow," said Mighty, impressed by their design.
chief planner asked: "Can you make a sign?"
"Mom and I," he boasted, "could easy make nine."
But how can we get 'em here, yet keep 'em fine"?

"You kite it back," said the planner with glee.
"Deliver it to me on shore," the manager wrote.
"Kiting is quicker," even Bertha could see.
"Be sure it is water-proof" called scapegoat.

Might jerked the fish line as signal to depart
His mother began pulling him in.
Bertha tossed her head to give him a start.
He kited right off like Errol Flynn.

"They want a 'No Smoking' sign
in exchange for dad's safety,"
he told his mother. This sounded benign
and they began to work frantically.

So it was that they made a large sign.
They used Varsol™ to keep it dry.
Might grabbed the sign, Mom the line
He kited low and fast back to Bertha's eye.

"It smells like cheese; I'm going to sneeze,"
said Bertha, lurching toward Might's dad.
The wind waited, dropping to a breeze
History's biggest sneeze was certain to be bad.

It darkened the sun, the wind it dissectionated.
It sprayed five or ten smoking fishermen,
from Bertha's mouth in all directions,
It blew Mighty's dad on shore, smooth as a new sedan

"Ho! Ho!" said Bertha. "What a relief. Thanks
Mighty. Mighty? Where is that clever lad?"
Not a trace! Not there! Not even on sea banks.
They found the raincoat—empty—looking sad.

They searched until it was dark as loam
and agreed to search tomorrow
Might's mom and dad and sister went home
each with dreadful thoughts of sorrow.

At home, the door was ajar
They entered. There at the table was Might,
one hand in the empty cookie jar.
"Hey Mom! What's for supper tonight?"

THE PIONEERS

SADDLES

They left the saddles to o'er winter
In the shed. No one would come by
But to porcupine with love of salt,
The saddles were his apple pie.

SEARCHING FOR BILBY

Sometime after the war
Bilby got lost, or just the door
Beside the Devil's Lake
By lore
The lake without a floor.

All roads lead some other way
My dad had courted there some say
I recently spent a day
And found only a tiny bay
In the Devil's lake

GRAVEYARD OF THE PIONEERS

Three children of the pioneers
Walked past the fixed-up church
Going quick to see where grandma lay
With daughters and a granddaughter

They found to their surprise a calming force
That set right the current hectic pace
And soon the graveyard was their place

They then searched for all their friends
With many dressed in granite
Closer than they'd been in years
Yet greeted with happiness and never tears

The ones who'd done them wrong
as welcome as their in-life friends

There were graves from a century ago
Someone had fixed up illegible names
Some names scratched in concrete
Some still with a simple wooden cross
And tiny graves with children's stories

A graveyard is a happy place.

HOMESTEADER'S DREAMS

They dreamed of space and rich homestead
A land of deep and fine dark fertile soil
It's true sometimes they had fled
To escape a past, even if it meant a life of toil

They wanted new life with a wider sense of worth.
While surveying land in response to every quest
We hear them now with their pride and broader girth.
Debating which of all the farms was best.

They filed on quarters chosen carefully,
And worked with family to clear and plow.
There were difficulties they were not problem free,
Short of lumber, they yet needed horse and cow.

Some had to learn how to sew, even to ride a horse

On the prairies hail put some on homeward route
And a few boreal trees were even worse.
But the greatest problem in the west was drought.

Palliser in 1857 had warned of dry years
For the Royal Society he walked the walk
but they wanted a scout with fewer fears.
The man said: Wheat, it's no place for livestock.

In London, Yankee claim jumpers were feared.
Get settlers near the border, justify the rail
Soil mattered little, settlers would not be heard.
Because the railroad could not fail.

But land and climate both were frail,
Settlers did not know what to do.
It took decades to see through the droughted veil,
And they were old before they knew.

Strip farms; at last some science.
With much more land and hopper bait.
But now the land act had fewer clients.
For most of them it was too late.

We see then even now as they close the gate
Leaving sagging roofs and doors windblown,
The burned-out barns their dreams update.
For in this land their lives were sown.

NOTE: *John Palliser explored the Canadian grasslands from Lake Superior to the Rocky Mountains in 1857-61. He found land suitable for agriculture along the Saskatchewan river valley. But found a vast area of drought, now called the Palliser's Triangle, roughly Calgary to Regina to Saskatoon. The Royal Society ignored his report, John Macoun a Canadian botanist wrote another report indicating low but timely rain suitable for growing wheat. But severe drought occurred 1929-1937. 13,900 settlers abandoned their holdings.*

OLD AGE: BE HAPPY

WHAT A LOAD

"You lied to me," spoken with dignity,
But his heart was pounding I could see.
While filling my cup with faculty brew,
He'd come over and I'd said, "How are you?"
His reply quite new was not my due:
"You lied to me."

It took a moment to recall,
I'd left his supervision in the fall.
That's how I knew it was exactly 40 years ago.

After I'd left, he phoned to ask:
Had I taken a case (errata) of student data.
I searched, then phoned him back.
"I don't think I've got it."
That's what I told him soft and low.
Understated not dramatic
I regretted not being more emphatic.

Now he was very old, I guess he needed to unload.
Putting his affairs in order.
Before he was called to cross the border,
I resisted the anger and the shouted denial,
It was I believed not me on trial.
He'd become a professor being too weak to farm,
I walked away intending him no further harm.

As I see it now, ordering his affairs
Meant he must unload his cares.
An idea he'd carried for so long,
Could it possibly be wrong?

You lied to me, almost in tears.
What could it mean after all those years?
Only later I'd come to see,
He'd passed his heavy load on to me.

He believed I'd done him wrong in wrath
I must carry this down my shortening path.
He believed I'd done him wrong
Believed it for so long.

DREAMS

There are things I want to do,
Laborious deeds I now eschew,
Trying to work in teams,
To accomplish those goals still in my dreams.

SLEEP

I take a lot of sleep,
It's comforting and it's cheap,
But often dreams go much too deep,
Sometimes regrets pile into a heap.

Forcing me to review errors
That I can't keep locked up all the time.

THE BITE OF TIME

A chastening trip to the graveyard of the pioneers,
Provides a lesson not of forms nor death.
But of the inexorable bite of time,
And how it cuts into eternity for everyone,
Destroying all people and all things in its wake.

STILL SOME OUTPUT

The ambient light now fading away,
Can't see as well as yesterday,
The sunlight seems to ration its streaming,
By 3 p.m. it's lost its gleaming,
Leaving long shadows over snowy lawns.

Still some output
I used a flashlight to see if a screw,
Was slotted, Robertson or Phillips.
This spells trouble and its new,
I'm thinking 'Take your time'.
Can't work as fast as yesteryear,
The work is slow the surfaces smear,
But here is still some output here.

MY NARRATIVE

A life's story comes and goes,
If one's alert it clearly grows,
Adding each day an extra chapter,
Without a sense of coming after.

My early chapters are oh so worn,
Packed with stories one would now scorn,
Full of events I'd as sooner forget.
Would they had not happened and yet
with what replace?

The middle chapters should carry on,
Instead they go from dusk to dawn.
They seem to tarry in midstream,
As though awakening from troubled dream.

The whole is full of evil foment,
Unfortunate events and troubling moments.
With consequences fowl and bitter,
'strike out' for the heavy hitter.

I'm going to edit my life story.
Take out the evil schemes and dreams of glory.
Remove the hero's selfish bent.
Pretend there were no grand intent.

With this new version I'll lie in peace,
And recriminations perhaps will finally cease.
Who cares if the story's dull as hell?
It's not a story I want to tell.

But wait, dull's never fun,
Success and winning outranks "never run."
If I add a little luck and skill
No need forever run myself downhill.

GOING BACK

Here is where we walked barefoot as children,
We squelched God's dust between our toes.
All people were our friends and brethren.
The complex tools were horse's shoes and garden hoes.
Today we are old and wiser far,
The childhood paths are wide roads now.
God's dust replaced by manmade tar.
I'd like to go barefoot again but I've forgotten how.

HOME FOREVER

After seventy years, three siblings returned,
To the farm that once was home forever.
They'd left, for country ignorance was spurned,
Seeking fact and theory to make them clever.
But facts are fact wherever you construe,
And theories have neither price nor charm.
The things they knew in their deep tissue,
Harked back to wisdom from the farm.

LANDSCAPES GONE

The roads were changed.
The walking trails through bush were gone.
The houses and barns rearranged.
The church had stilled its song.
But something about the landscape,
with all its change is wrong.

COUNTRY SCHOOL HOUSE

The old schoolhouse completely gone.
Instead a gravel pit.
Left them feeling so forlorn,
Their memories did not fit.

WHAT IS MANAGEABLE WHEN YOU ARE OLD?

We do not want the long-lost past too close

The past: too painful leave it undisturbed.
Just recall the sound, the smells, the sights so vast,
And confirm how memories similar cast,
Enough to say it using careful word.
Be there, but not too close,
Be spectators not participants. Like running with the bulls.

Three old sibs, approaching death, came together for
   the day.
One made a joke of everything, yet seemed oblivious
   to pain.
One so defeated by life itself, he could not laugh at all.
A third with something yet to prove, always right,
   always to the wall.

GRAVEYARD

We who for the moment, walk above ground:
We paragons of regret.
What wisdom do we have in store?
What debts are still to pay?

WHEN YOU ARE OLD

When you are old and grey and full of sleep,
Hold to the blue of bird or smell of flower,
And so rebuild your dreams when life was deep,
Then in the confines o' your lover's bower,
Adoration led you on to health and power.
That was a time when youth was full of trust,
Before trust betrayed decayed to lust, and quickly dust.

Note: First line from Yeats

REMEMBER ME

Above the broad river's sweep,
A sheltered cove with a wooden seat,
Beckons the walker who travels alone
With a tiny plaque and a name unknown.
Date of birth and death for both are free.
The little plaque said, "Sometimes remember me."

Was he some giant or a man of science
Or a commanding warrior who lived defiant?

Sit on the seat he must have bought,
As the river fades because of his thought,
Remember me daughter, remember me son;
And yes remember me mom!
Not a scholar or a Genghis Khan,
Just a father, a son, and a loving man.

Plaque of Nick Delker on the North Saskatchewan River at Edmonton

COVID-19 A NON-THINKING CREATURE

A non-thinking creature drifted by.
It does not think, it does not plan.
It does not see; it has no eye.
Dumber than the wars of man.
It cannot fly—just drifted by.
We are so afraid we quake and cry.
Inhaling, we unthinking, breathe him in.
Afraid of that tiny inside guy? I'll tell you why.
It is made of human DNA: has keys to all mankind.
Cough? we spew out more infectious kin.
It evolves so fast, that vaccines must start behind.
And that is why we quake and cry: why we fear him.

BE HAPPY

Do not stand at my grave and moan.
I am not there; It's not my home.
Besides moaning is not the thing to do,
Because I'm better off than you.
And though there are difficulties galore,
Mosquitoes don't bite me anymore.

I don't have to laugh at the bosses' jokes
Nor be polite to your rude folks.
I don't kiss grubby kids,
I'm no longer afraid of SIDS.
I don't make time for any bore,
And mosquitoes don't bite me anymore.

I don't write exams world ills to cure,
I never have to call men: 'sir'.
Neither celebrities nor power impress,
There is no need for me to jest,
My food like squirrels I need not store,
And mosquitoes don't bite me anymore.

JAPANESE-STYLE POETRY

HAIKU

All animals die
Accident or disease
Or is it murder?

Drilling mud
Death is universal
You walked through boiling mud
Did you want to die?

KATUATAS

Is a baby perfect?
Give it eighty years of wear.
Systems fail, the grave awaits.

What does the mother see?
Only the twinkle in its eye
As proof of immortality.

TANKA

The Gods are smiling
They promise
High yields and good price
Mom earned her rest.
No one forecast hail and snow
But mom has gone to rest.

WAKA

Opening the empty bin
I found a swallow's nest
Sometimes life is cruel
Death served as random event
Must I execute its fate?

CONCLUSION

Poets try to balance original and profound thought against a surprising or creative presentation.

Leonard Cohen wrote:

> "Forget your perfect offering,
> There is a crack in everything.
> That's how the light gets in."

We thus learn that imperfection begats wisdom. Cohen uses "light" to denote information or knowledge and leans it on the inevitability of imperfection.

Robert Frost uses a play on words:

> "I took the road less traveled by.
> And that has made all the difference."

But we know, if the standards are loose, any little thing will "make all the difference."

Thomas Gray would not settle for imperfection and penned a perfect stanza to a lost love:

> The curfew tolls the knell of parting day,
> The lowing herd winds slowly o'er the lea
> The plowman homeward wends his weary way
> And leaves the world to darkness **and** to me.

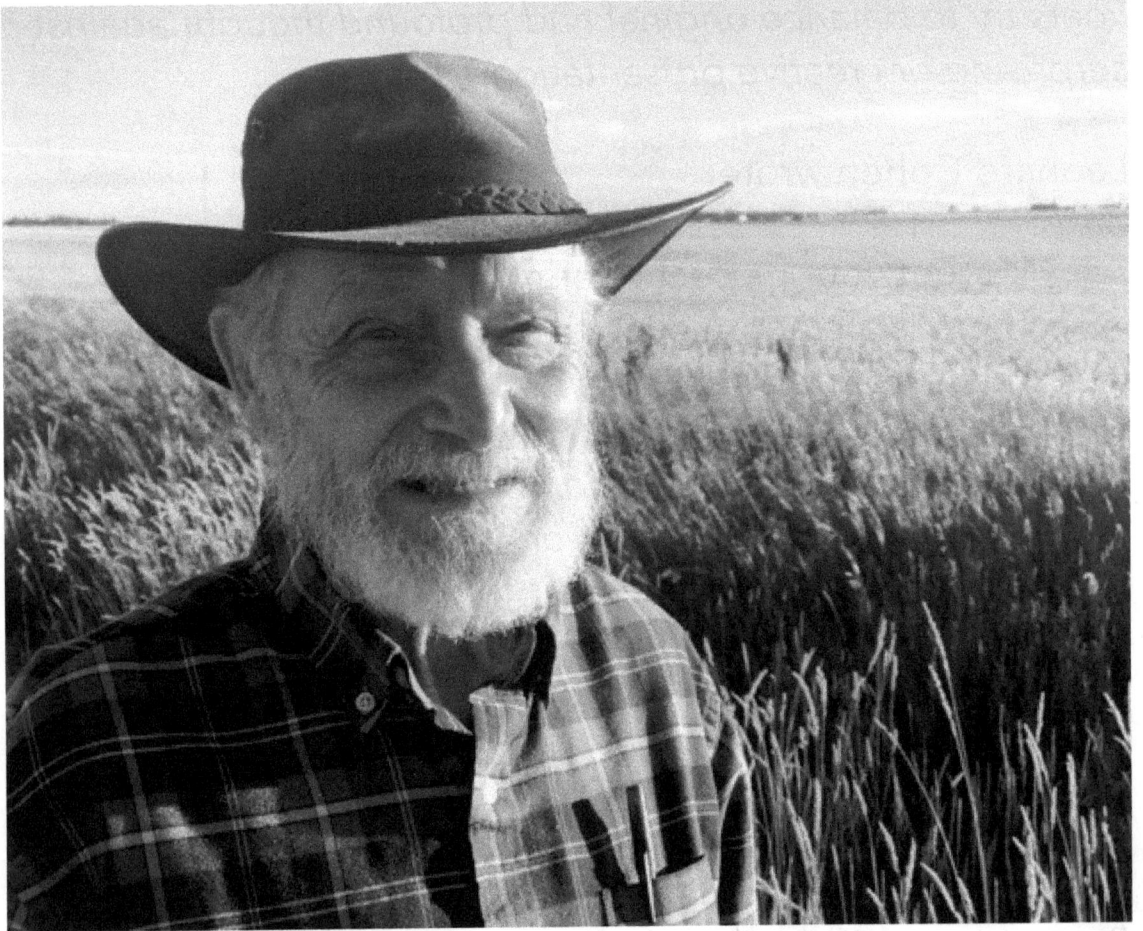

ABOUT THE AUTHOR

Dr. George Winter was born in 1930 in Heatherdown, Alberta, Canada. His life began on a desperately poor farm surrounded by equally poor farm neighbors during the Great Depression. His mother, Lena Laverty, was a teacher but lost her job when she married his father, Robert Winter, as was customary at that time.

Lena had moved from New Brunswick to escape the damp climate which triggered her asthma. But the dry, cold Alberta climate and farm dust made things worse. George heard his mother gasping for life on many cold, wintery nights. He feared each breath might be her last.

Two uncles bought a team of horses for his father, and that enabled Robert to grow potatoes for a crew working the nearby gravel pit.

George studied at the Vermilion School of Agriculture (now Lakeland College), the University of Alberta, and Iowa State University, and UBC. He spent most of his career in college administration—though he really preferred teaching.

Only after retiring did he find time to write a little poetry. Now 90 years old, his eyesight and hearing fade. But he still walks, bicycles, writes, and repairs farm machinery. Here he reflects on the broad sweep of life—the good times and the bad.

Life is full of twists and turns. Whatever bends in the road you are facing in your own life today, perhaps this book will provide a fresh and historic perspective. Thanks for reading it.

www.ingramcontent.com/pod-product-compliance
Lightning Source LLC
Chambersburg PA
CBHW081250040426

42452CB00015B/2773

9780972249775